Diarmuid Brittain

CCEA GCSE
FRENCH VOCABULARY BOOK 4

Verbs, Conjunctions & Other Useful Phrases

COLOURPOINT EDUCATIONAL

© Diarmuid Brittain and Colourpoint Creative Ltd 2022

ISBN: 978 1 78073 344 9

First Edition
First impression

Layout and design: April Sky Design
Printed by: GPS Colour Graphics Ltd, Belfast

All rights reserved. No part of this publication may be reproduced, stored in a retrieval system or transmitted in any form or by any means, electronic, mechanical, photocopying, scanning, recording or otherwise, without the prior written permission of the copyright owners and publisher of this book.

Copyright has been acknowledged to the best of our ability. If there are any inadvertent errors or omissions, we shall be happy to correct them in any future editions.

The Author

Diarmuid Brittain taught French for 26 years at Grosvenor Grammar School, Belfast. He is also an A level French Examiner for an awarding body.

He lives with his wife and three children in Belfast and remains a Francophile through and through.

This book has borrowed inspiration from hundreds of pupils over the years and it is dedicated to each and every language student and teacher that has graced the doors of Grosvenor Grammar School.

Colourpoint Educational
An imprint of Colourpoint Creative Ltd
Colourpoint House
Jubilee Business Park
21 Jubilee Road
Newtownards
County Down
Northern Ireland
BT23 4YH

Tel: 028 9182 0505
E-mail: sales@colourpoint.co.uk
Website: www.colourpoint.co.uk

This book has been written to help students preparing for the GCSE French specification from CCEA. While Colourpoint Educational and the author have taken every care in its production, we are not able to guarantee that the book is completely error-free. Additionally, while the book has been written to closely match the CCEA specification, it is the responsibility of each candidate to satisfy themselves that they have fully met the requirements of the CCEA specification prior to sitting an exam set by that body. For this reason, and because specifications change with time, we strongly advise every candidate to avail of a qualified teacher and to check the contents of the most recent specification for themselves prior to the exam. Colourpoint Educational therefore cannot be held responsible for any errors or omissions in this book or any consequences thereof.

Contents

	Introduction	**4**
1:	**Les verbes les plus importants**	**6**
	(The most important verbs) – alphabetically ordered by French	
2:	**La colle française (les connecteurs)**	**35**
	(French glue – the connectors)	

Introduction

This is one of four books that form a resource for English-speaking students of French and which seeks to promote **student-led vocabulary acquisition**. It is designed to **promote independent learning** and **free up teacher time**. While it is tailored for GCSE students, it is a powerful resource for all English-speaking students of French.

What do the books cover?

Various GCSE French syllabi (CCEA, WJEC, Edexcel, AQA, OCR) have common vocabulary lists. While this resource makes specific reference to the CCEA specification, it covers the vocabulary listed in all these syllabi and can be used with all of them.

The resource is divided into four books, the first three of which cover the three areas of core vocabulary as presented in the GCSE syllabi:
1. Identity, Lifestyle and Culture
2. Local, National, International and Global Areas of Interest
3. School Life, Studies and the World of Work

The resource is completed by a fourth book (this book):
4. Verbs, Conjunctions and Other Useful Phrases, which includes an alphabetical list of the most common verbs in French, as well as a list of common connectors, *la Colle Française* (French glue).

Why these books?
- These books are designed to be used independently by students.
- Traditionally, students have been given lists of vocabulary to learn without pronunciation guides and without *aide-mémoires*. With these books, teachers can hand vocabulary learning over to their students, giving the teacher more time to focus on the challenging grammar that requires teacher-led pedagogy.
- Research shows that pupils prefer to learn from hard copies.
- Pupils can have a sense of ownership of this a resource because they can annotate it.
- The most recent GCSE CCEA specification (first examined in 2017) places more emphasis on Listening and Reading, demanding a higher level of vocabulary acquisition.
- This resource can be used independently by students from Year 8 onwards, building over five years to GCSE success. This is particularly useful for schools that need to use remote learning from time to time.

What is the structure of this book?

The vocabulary in the book is presented in the same order as it is presented in the CCEA GCSE syllabus, i.e. in alphabetical order by the English meaning.

Each word has a **pronunciation guide**. The benefits of this are the following:

- Learners can check their pronunciation of the word.
- Learners can test understanding from looking only at the pronunciation guide, thereby improving their listening skills.
- Learners can test themselves on how to write – in correct French – the phonetically described word, thereby improving the accuracy of their writing.
- Learners can work in pairs to test each other orally from English to French and/or French to English.

Most words also have an ***aide-mémoire***. *Aide-mémoire* is French for 'memory aid'. People often struggle under the burden of learning vocabulary, and take little pleasure from the task.

It is the author's belief that if a student can find links between their own language and a foreign one, it makes the process of vocabulary acquisition more of a journey of discovery than a drudgery, and importantly, it allows the learner to hook the foreign words onto words that have already been assimilated in their brain.

The author likes to work with the premise 'words can make you laugh!' There are a number of attempts to be humorous throughout the book, in an effort to link works to the mind of the student. Learners may describe these attempts as 'dad jokes' – but the author believes that learners secretly like them!

The book also includes sections entitled **Practise!** These allow students to practise what they have learned, embedding their learning. Teachers will also find these sections useful in order to set homework or cover work.

What are the tick boxes for?

Each word has three tick boxes. These are provided in order to give the student a way to track their progress and organise their learning. The author suggests the following approach, though you can use whatever method works for you:

- Tick the first box when you have learned the word for the first time. When you are organising your revision use this tick to indicate to yourself what you have covered.
- When you come back later to check that you have retained the word, you can tick the second box.
- By the time you go in to your GCSE exams, you should have been able to tick the third box, to show that you have embedded that word in your brain.

Abbreviations

The book uses the following abbreviations:

(m)	masculine	e.g. *Un garçon*, a boy
(f)	feminine	e.g. *Une fille*, a girl
(m/f)	masculine or feminine	e.g. *Un/une professeur*, a teacher
(mpl)	masculine plural	e.g. *Des garçons*, (some) boys
(fpl)	feminine plural	e.g. *Des filles*, (some) girls

1: Les verbes les plus importants
(The most important verbs – alphabetically ordered by French)

Note: Not all parts of every verb are given because you don't need them if you know the following rules for the present tense:

1. If the *je* part ends in **e**, then the rule for *il/elle* is as shown in this example:
   Je jou**e** → Il/Elle jou**e**

2. If the *je* part ends in **ds** or **cs**, then the rule for *il/elle* is as shown in these examples:
   Je ven**ds** → Il/Elle ven**d**
   Je convain**cs** → Il/Elle convain**c**

3. If the *je* part ends in **is**, **rs**, **ts** or **ns**, then the rule for *il/elle* is as shown in these examples:
   Je cro**is** → Il cro**it**
   Je so**rs** → Il so**rt**
   Je me**ts** → Il me**t**
   J'attei**ns** → Il attein**t**
   (Note: the *il/elle* part **never** ends in **s**.)

4. The *tu* part always ends in **s**, apart from two exceptions, 'tu veux' (you want) and 'tu peux' (you can).

5. If the *nous* part ends in **ons**, then the *vous* part ends in **ez**. The only exceptions are 'nous faisons' (vous faites), 'nous disons' (vous dîtes) and 'nous sommes' (vous êtes).

6. The *ils* part and the *elles* part are the same and always end in **nt** (most often ending in **ent**).

7. Irregular subjunctive forms are noted in brackets.

Word or phrase	Key forms of the verb	Aide-mémoire	English meaning	Check
Abandonner	J'abandonne, nous abandonnons, ils abandonnent, j'abandonnerai, j'ai abandonné,	Abandon the ship, give it up	Abandon, give up	
Absenter, s'	Je m'absente, nous nous absentons, ils s'absentent, je m'absenterai, je me suis absenté(e)	Absent oneself	Absent oneself, stay away	
Accepter	J'accepte, nous acceptons, ils acceptent, j'accepterai, j'ai accepté		Accept	
Accompagner	J'accompagne, nous accompagnons, ils accompagnent, j'accompagnerai, j'ai accompagné		Accompany	
Acheter	J'achète, nous achetons, ils achètent, j'achèterai, j'ai acheté	A pur**cha**se is linked. 'I bought an **acht**r**ay** and then I stopped smoking'. What an idiot!	Buy	
Admirer	J'admire, nous admirons, ils admirent, j'admirerai, j'ai admiré		Admire	

LES VERBES LES PLUS IMPORTANTS

Word or phrase	Key forms of the verb	Aide-mémoire	English meaning	Check
Adopter	J'adopte, nous adoptons, ils adoptent, j'adopterai, j'ai adopté		Adopt	
Adorer	J'adore, nous adorons, ils adorent, j'adorerai, j'ai adoré		Love, worship	
Affluer	J'afflue, nous affluons, ils affluent, j'affluerai, j'ai afflué	Flood in, flow in. A **flu**x is a flow, a rush.	Rush in	
Agir	J'agis, il agit, nous agissons, ils agissent, j'agirai, j'ai agi	To **agi**tate is to act in an **agi**tating way	Act	
Agir, s… de, Il s'agit de	Il s'agit de, agissons, agissent, il s'agira de, il s'est agi de	Literally 'it acts itself of', e.g. 'It acts itself of working' – il s'agit de travailler, 'it's about working'.	It's about	
Aider	J'aide, nous aidons, ils aident, j'aiderai, j'ai aidé	Aid	Help	
Aimer	J'aime, nous aimons, ils aiment, j'aimerai, j'ai aimé	Amiable is kind, you like your ami, friend	Like, love	
Ajouter comme ami	J'ajoute *Sam* comme ami, nous ajoutons, ils ajoutent, j'ajouterai, j'ai ajouté	An adjunct is something that is added on. **A**jou**t**er, **a**ddi**t**ion.	Add (as a friend)	
Aller bien	Je vais, tu vas, il/elle va, nous allons, ils vont, j'irai, je suis allé (aille, ailles, allions, aillent)	Go down the **alle**y. Benign, benefit, benevolent. Ben is good, well.	Go well	
Aller à la pêche	Je vais, tu vas, il/elle va, nous allons, ils vont, j'irai, je suis allé (aille, ailles, allions, aillent)	Go down the **alle**y. Pêche – Poseidon (Greek God of the Sea), pisces (zodiac sign, fish), **pes**catarian.	Go fishing	
Allumer	J'allume, j'ai allumé	To illuminate, light up, switch on	Switch on	
Améliorer	J'améliore, nous améliorons, ils améliorent, j'améliorerai, j'ai amélioré	To ameliorate is to improve. Meilleur – better (make better – ameliorate). Meilleur ami – bestie.	Improve	
Amuser, s'…	Je m'amuse, nous nous amusons, ils s'amusent, je m'amuserai, je me suis amusé	Amuse, amusement	Have a good time	
Annuler	J'annule, il annule, nous annulons, ils annulent, j'annulerai, j'ai annulé	If you annul a marriage, you cancel it	Cancel	
Apparaître	J'apparaîs, il apparaît, nous apparaissons, ils apparaissent, j'apparaîtrai, j'ai apparu	Apparition, appearance	Appear	
Appeler, s'…	Je m'appelle, nous nous appelons, ils s'appellent, je m'appelerai, je me suis appelé	To appeal to someone is to call to them	Call, be called	
Apprécier	J'apprécie, nous apprécions, ils apprécient, j'apprécierai, j'ai apprécié		Appreciate	

7

Word or phrase	Key forms of the verb	Aide-mémoire	English meaning	Check
Apprendre	J'apprends, il apprend, nous apprenons, ils apprennent, j'apprendrai, j'ai appris	Apprentices are employed to learn	Learn	
Arranger	J'arrange, nous arrangeons, ils arrangent, j'arrangerai, j'ai arrangé		Arrange	
Arrêter	J'arrête, nous arrêtons, ils arrêtent, j'arrêterai, j'ai arrêté,	ê denotes an 's' after the ê. Cardiac arrest. The police stop or arrest.	Stop	
Arriver	J'arrive, nous arrivons, ils arrivent, j'arriverai, je suis arrivé		Arrive, happen	
Arriver à faire quelque chose	J'arrive à, nous arrivons à, ils arrivent à, j'arriverai à, je suis arrivé à	Arrive at the point where you can do something	Manage to do something	
Assister à	J'assiste, nous assistons, ils assistent, j'assisterai, j'ai assisté	A lady in waiting **attends** to her mistress or **assist**s her mistress	Attend (a concert)	
Assurer	J'assure, j'ai assuré	Assure, link to insure, I assure you, you are insured	Insure	
Attacher	J'attache, j'ai attaché		Attach	
Attaquer	J'attaque, nous arrivons, ils arrivent, j'attaquerai, j'ai attaqué		Attack	
Atteindre	J'atteins, il atteint, nous atteignons, ils atteignent, j'atteindrai, j'ai atteint	**Att**a**in**, to attain a certain standard	Reach	
Attendre	J'attends, il attend, nous attendons, ils attendent, j'attendrai, j'ai attendu	If a lady in **wait**ing is **attend**ing to her mistress, she is doing her job	Wait	
Atterrir	J'atterris, il atterrit, nous atterrissons, ils atterrissent, j'atterrirai, j'ai atterri	Terre – territory, terrain, ground, earth. À – to. Aterrir, – to go to the terrain, to go to the ground.	Land	
Attraper	J'attrape, nous attrapons, ils attrapent, j'attraperai, j'ai attrapé	To **trap** with your hands	Catch	
Augmenter	J'augmente, nous augmentons, ils augmentent, j'augmenterai, j'ai augmenté	To augment my earnings is to increase my earnings	Increase	
Autoriser à faire	J'autorise, nous autorisons, ils autorisent, j'autoriserai, j'ai autorisé	To **auth**o**rise** is to allow	Allow	
Avoir, ai, avons, ont	J'ai, tu as, il/elle a, nous avons, ils ont, j'aurai, j'ai eu (aie, aies, ait, ayons, ayez, aient)	Birds 'av-wire' under their claws	Have	

Word or phrase	Key forms of the verb	Aide-mémoire	English meaning	Check
Avoir besoin	J'ai besoin, j'ai eu besoin	Bees **need** to bizz wah(n) they work	Need	
Avoir chaud	J'ai chaud	Chauffer – to heat (**ca**lor gas for heating). A chauffeur used to warm the car up.	Be warm	
Avoir faim	J'ai faim	**Fam**ished is very hungry, also **fam**ine	Be hungry	
Avoir froid	J'ai froid	Here we have cold, froid, **frid**ge	Be cold	
Avoir lieu	Ça a lieu	Ça a lieu tous les samedis – It takes place every Saturday. A tenant holds the house, a lieutenant holds the place. Time off in lieu means time off in place of pay. In lieu of, in place of.	Take place	
Avoir soif	J'ai soif	To qua**ff** (could be spelt **c**oif in French, oi = wa) is to drink in big gulps	Be thristy	
Avoir mal à…	J'ai mal à la tête – I have a sore head, il a mal au (à + le = au) bras – he has a sore arm, nous avons mal aux (à + les = aux) dents, ils ont mal à l'épaule – they have a sore shoulder (yep, just one between them all)	**Mal**practice, **mal**nourished. **Mal** – bad, here means sickness. I have sickness at… – J'ai mal à…	Sore, to have a sore…	
Avoir mal au cœur	J'ai mal au coeur	**Mal**practice, **mal**nourished, **mal** – badness, sickness. Au coeur – at the heart, **core** of an apple (heart of the apple), **car**diac (referencing the heart). Mal au coeur – sickness at the heart actually means to feel nauseous.	Sick (nauseous), to feel	
Avoir raison	J'ai raison	Have r**eason** on your side, be **reason**able	Be right	
Avoir tort	J'ai tort	A legal **tort** is a crime. **Tort**ure is also wrong.	Be wrong	
Avoir peur	J'ai peur	**Pe**t**r**ified, scared	Be afraid	
Avoir le droit de faire quelque chose	J'ai le droit de faire quelque chose	Droit – if you are adroit you are upright. Chose – my thing, my choice. 'Cosa nostra', 'our thing', motto of the Mafia.	Have the right to do something	
Avoir l'intention de faire quelque chose	J'ai l'intention de faire quelque chose	To have the intention of doing something	Intend to do something	
Avoir envie de faire quelque chose	J'ai envie de	To **envy** or desire, to have envy, desire, to do something	Want (have desire)	

GCSE FRENCH VOCABULARY BOOK 4 – VERBS, CONJUNCTIONS & OTHER USEFUL PHRASES

Word or phrase	Key forms of the verb	Aide-mémoire	English meaning	Check
Avoir hâte de faire quelque chose	J'ai hâte de	â denotes an 's' after the a, therefore haste, to have haste to do something	Really want to do something	
Avouer	J'avoue, nous avouons, ils avouent, j'avouerai, j'ai avoué	To make **a vow** is to confess	Confess, admit	
Bavarder	Je bavarde, nous bavardons, ils bavardent, je bavarderai, j'ai bavardé	Ba ba bavarder, **bla**, **bla**, **bla**b on about, **b**leat, **ba**bble on, all talking	Chat	
Blesser	Je blesse, nous blessons, ils blessent, je blesserai, j'ai blessé	Aaaachoo! Bless you! You are injured with the flu. You need blessed when you are injured.	Injure	
Blesser, se	Je me blesse, je me suis blessé	Aaaachoo! Bless you! You are injured with the flu. You need blessed when you are injured.	Injure one**self**	
Boire	Je bois, nous buvons, ils boivent, je boirai, j'ai bu	**B**everage, **bo**ttle, **boi**ling water	Drink	
Border	Je borde, j'ai bordé	Fold in the **border**, the edge	Tuck in	
Boucher	Je bouche, j'ai bouché	A **bouch**on is a cork blocking the mouth of the bottle. A **bu**t**che**r puts food in your mouth to block it up.	Block	
Bouger	Je bouge, il bouge, nous bougeons, ils bougent, je bougerai, j'ai bougé	A **boog**ie on the dance floor is all about your 'moves'	To move	
Briller	Je brille, j'ai brillé	**Brill**iant means shining brightly	Shine	
Bronzer	Je bronze, j'ai bronzé	Becoming **bronzed**	Tan	
Brosser	Je brosse, j'ai brossé		Brush	
Calculer	Je calcule, j'ai calculé		Calculate	
Camper	Je campe, il campe	Camper – link to camping	Camp	
Casser	Je casse, j'ai cassé	**Cas**t off (break off) your chains and be free!	Break	
Causer	Je cause, j'ai causé		Cause	
Causer	Je cause, j'ai causé	Have a **cos**y **ch**at	Chat	
Changer	Je change, j'ai changé		Change	
Chanter	Je chante, j'ai chanté	**Chant** – to sing, especially at a football match	Sing	
Chercher	Je cherche, j'ai cherché	Chercher, s**ear**ch	Look for, pick up	
Choisir	Je choisis, il choisit, nous choisissons, ils choisissent, je choisirai, j'ai choisi	Choice	Choose	
Chômer	Je chôme, j'ai chômé	'Shô' me what to do	Be unemployed	
Choquer	Je choque, j'ai choqué		Shock	

LES VERBES LES PLUS IMPORTANTS

Word or phrase	Key forms of the verb	Aide-mémoire	English meaning	Check
Cliquer	Je clique, J'ai cliqué		Click	
Cocher	Je coche, j'ai coché	The **co**a**ch** ticks you off the list if you have worked, if not, he ticks you off!	Tick	
Coiffer	Je coiffe, j'ai coiffé	**Quiff**	Do hair	
Commander	Je commande, j'ai commandé	To command is to order	Order	
Commencer	Je commence, j'ai commencé	Commence, start, begin	Start, begin	
Comparer	Je compare, j'ai comparé		Compare	
Compléter	Je complète, j'ai complété		Complete	
Composter	Je composte, j'ai composté	To punch a ticket. It actually means to punch a hole, with the little circular piece of paper being punched out. One could put all those little round bits in a compost heap.	Punch (a ticket)	
Compter sur	Je compte sur, j'ai compté sur	**Co**mp**t**er – **co**u**n**t on a counter	Count on	
Comprendre	Je comprends, il comprend, nous comprenons, ils comprennent, je comprendrai, j'ai compris	Comprehension is all about understanding	Understand	
Conduire	Je conduis, il conduit, nous conduisons, ils conduisent, je conduirai, j'ai conduit	To **condu**ct an orchestra is to **drive** the performance	Drive	
Connaître	Je connaîs, il connaît, nous connaissons, ils connaissent, je connaîtrai, j'ai connu	Conscious of, cognescent both 'aware', reconnaissance to gain knowledge	Know (person)	
Consacrer, se...	Je consacre, j'ai consacré, je me consacre, je me suis consacré	**To cons**e**cr**ate some ground to a church is to devote it to the church	Devote (oneself)	
Conseiller	Je conseille, j'ai conseillé	**Cou**n**sell**ors give **cou**n**sel**, they advise	Advise	
Conserver	Je conserve, j'ai conservé	Conserve	Keep	
Contacter	Je contacte, j'ai contacté		Contact	
Contaminer	Je contamine, j'ai contaminé		Contaminate	
Continuer	Je continue, j'ai continué		Continue	
Contribuer	Je contribue, j'ai contribué		Contribute	
Copier	Je copie, j'ai copié		Copy	
Corriger	Je corrige, j'ai corrigé	Corriger – **corr**ect	Correct	
Courir	Je cours, il court, nous courons, ils courent, je courrai, j'ai couru	Couriers run messages. A race course where you run.	Run	
Coûter	Je coûte, j'ai coûté	û denotes 's' after the û, therefore **co**u**st**er	Cost	
Créer	Je crée, J'ai créé		Create	

11

Word or phrase	Key forms of the verb	Aide-mémoire	English meaning	Check
Critiquer	Je critique, j'ai critiqué	Critiques criticise	Criticise	
Cuisiner	Je cuisine, j'ai cuisiné	Cuisine is cooking in France. It also means kitchen.	Cook	
Cultiver	Je cultive, j'ai cultivé	Cultiver – cultivate	Cultivate	
Danser	Je danse, j'ai dansé	Careful, dance from the 'c' to the 's'	Dance	
Débarasser la table	Je débarasse, j'ai débarassé	Embarrassed means being stuck with an awkward problem. Débarassé means having got rid of it.	Clear the table (get rid of the dirty dishes)	
Débrancher	Je débranche, j'ai débranché	De **branch** is plugged in to the limb, like a plug in a wall. Unplug it.	Unplug	
Décevoir	Je déçois, il déçoit, nous décevons, ils déçoivent, je décevrai, j'ai déçu	Looks like but is not 'to deceive'! Disappointing, isn't it?	Disappoint	
Décider	Je décide, j'ai décidé		Decide	
Déclarer	Je déclare, j'ai déclaré		Declare	
Décoller	Je décolle, j'ai décollé	A collage is a picture created by **sticking** items on a canvass or a wall. Coller – the verb, to stick. 'dé' reverses the meaning, so here, to unstick. A plane unsticks itself from the ground when it takes off.	Take off (airplane)	
Décorer	Je décore, j'ai décoré		Decorate	
Décourager	Je décourage, j'ai découragé		Discourage, put off	
Découvrir	Je découvre, il découvre, nous découvrons, ils découvrent, je découvrirai, j'ai découvert		Discover	
Décrire	Je décris, il décrit, nous décrivons, ils décrivent, je décrirai, j'ai décrit		Describe	
Déguster	Je déguste, j'ai dégusté	Strangely this looks like it would mean, 'disgust'. Ironically, it is the complete opposite, 'to savour' or 'to taste' as in wine-tasting. To taste in order to test.	Taste (wine-tasting)	
Déjeuner	Je déjeune, j'ai déjeuné	Jeûner – to fast. Jenny's fast! To break fast (breakfast) is déjeuner. However, breakfast is actually le petit-déjeuner and to have **lunch** is déjeuner.	Lunch, to have lunch	
Demander	Je demande, j'ai demandé	To demand something of someone is to ask forcefully	Ask	

LES VERBES LES PLUS IMPORTANTS

Word or phrase	Key forms of the verb	Aide-mémoire	English meaning	Check
Demander, se	Je me demande, je me suis demandé	Demand, to ask forcefully, to ask one**se**lf, to wonder.	Wonder (to one**se**lf)	
Déménager	Je déménage, j'ai déménagé	A 'ménage à trois' is a household of three, to un-household (dé-ménager) is to move.	Move house	
Démontrer	Je démontre, j'ai démontré		Demonstrate	
Dépendre de	Je dépends de, il dépend de, nous dépendons, ils dépendent, je dépendrai, j'ai dépendu de		Depend	
Dépenser	Je dépense, j'ai dépensé	To dispense with money is to get rid of it, spend it	Spend money	
Se déplacer	Je me déplace, je me suis déplacé	To **d**is**place** one**se**lf is to move about	Move about	
Déplier	Je déplie, j'ai déplié	A pleat is a fold, to unpleat is to unfold	Unfold	
Descendre	Je descends, il descend, nous descendons, ils descendent, je descendrai, je suis descendu	Descend, to go down	Go down	
Dessiner	Je dessine, j'ai dessiné	**Desi**gn – draw	Draw	
Détendre, se	Je me détends, il se détend, nous nous détendons, ils se détendent, je me détendrai, je me suis détendu	'De' as a prefix (i.e. at the start of a word) reverses the meaning. **Ten**dre – to **ten**se, stretch. Hence détendre – to de-tense, to relax.	Relax	
Détester	Je déteste, j'ai détesté	Detest, to hate	Hate	
Détruire	Je détruis, il détruit, nous détruisons, ils détruisent, je détruirai, j'ai détruit	**De**st**r**oy	Destroy	
Devenir membre d'un club	Je deviens, il devient, nous devenons, ils deviennent, je deviendrai, je suis devenu	Venir – to come, **come** to the **ven**ue. Also, what **comes** back to you when you work? Re**venue**. This verb, devenir is therefore like de-come, which is like become.	Become member of a club	
Devoir	Je dois, il doit, nous devons, ils doivent, je devrai, j'ai dû	**D**evoir also means **d**uty. One **has to** do one's duty.	Have to, to have to, must	
Dîner	Je dîne, j'ai dîné	Diner is very similar to dinner	Dine, have dinner	
Dire	Je dis, il dit, nous disons, vous dîtes, ils disent, je dirai, j'ai dit	Dire, diction, dictionary, words, tell, say	Say, tell	
Diriger	Je dirige, j'ai dirigé	**Dir**ect, **dir**iger	Direct	
Discuter	Je discute, j'ai discuté		Discuss	
Disparaître	Je disparais, il disparaît, nous disparaissons, ils disparaissent, je dispiraîtrai, j'ai disparu		Disappear	

13

Word or phrase	Key forms of the verb	Aide-mémoire	English meaning
Disputer, se	Je me dispute, je me suis disputé	Dispute, argue	Argue
Distribuer	Je distribue, j'ai distribué	**Distribu**te – distribuer. Be careful, the French has no 't'.	Distribute
Divorcer	Je divorce, J'ai divorcé		Divorce
Donner	Je donne, j'ai donné	**Don**ation is something you give	Give
Droguer, se	Je me drogue, je me suis drogué	**Drog**ue – **drug**, to drug one**se**lf is to take drugs	To take drugs
Durer	Je dure, j'ai duré	The **dur**ation of something is how long it lasts	Last
Échanger	J'échange, nous échangeons, ils échangent, j'échangerai, j'ai échangé		Exchange
Échouer	J'échoue, j'ai échoué	If you have échoues (pronounced 'ay shoes', sounds like 'issues'), you might fail!	Fail, do badly
Économiser	J'économise, j'ai economisé	Economise	Save money
Écouter	J'écoute, j'ai écouté	É denotes 's' and if you are a scout, you have your ear to the ground, listening. Listening to the echoes.	Listen
Écrire des lignes	J'écris, il écrit, nous écrivons, ils écrivent, j'écrirai, j'ai écrit	É denotes 's'. A scribe writes Scripture.	Write lines
Éditer	J'édite, j'ai édité	Editer – edit	Edit
Effacer	J'efface, j'ai effacé	Self-effacing means that you wipe away any overt pride. Also, the opposite, to deface, means that you write something on a surface which shouldn't be written on.	Rub out, delete
Éloigner, s'	J'éloigne, j'ai éloigné / je m'éloigne, je me suis éloigné	Hidden in éloigner is the word 'loin' which means a **lon**g way from, far	Move away
Emballer	J'emballe, j'ai emballé	Wrap up into a **ball**	Wrap up
Emmener	J'emmène, j'ai emmené	A **man**ager is a leader who brings someone with them, em**men**er	Bring someone
Empêcher	J'empêche, j'ai empêché	If the president is a bad boy, he must be **prevented** from being the president. He must be **impe**a**ched**.	Prevent
Emporter	J'emporte, j'ai emporté	Porters carry luggage. **Em** is a prefix which means 'away'. Carry and bring is to carry out and away.	Carry out/ take away

Word or phrase	Key forms of the verb	Aide-mémoire	English meaning
Emprunter	J'emprunte, j'ai emprunté	**Em** is a prefix which means 'away'. To **imp**o**und** means to hold, without owning. This is like borrowing.	Borrow
Enchaîner	J'enchaîne, j'ai enchaîné	A chain has links, links in a chain	Link with
Encourager	J'encourage, j'ai encouragé		Encourage
Enlever	J'enlève, j'ai enlevé	E**lev**ate is to lift up off, take off	Take off (clothes)
Enregistrer	J'enregistre, j'ai enregistré	To **register** a preference is to record a preference	Record
Enseigner	J'enseigne, j'ai enseigné	En**seig**ner. To **sign**post, or to show the way, is to teach.	Teach
Entendre	J'entends, il entend, nous entendons, ils entendent, j'entendrai, j'ai entendu	An **enten**te is when people **hear** each other, understand each other and get on	Hear
Entendre s'	Je m'entends, il s'entend, nous nous entendons, ils s'entendent, je m'entendrai, je me suis entendu	An **enten**te is when people hear each other, understand each other and **get on**	Get on with
Entrer	J'entre, je suis entré(e)	Entrer links to enter, go in	Enter, go in
Entretenir	J'entretiens, il entretient, nous entretenons, ils entretiennent, j'entretiendrai, j'ai entretenu	The ending, '**tain**' is linked to **tenir**, meaning to 'hold' (in good condition) by i**nter**vening with your hands (mains). **Main** as in **man**ipulate with hands.	Maintain
Entraîner	J'entraîne, j'ai entraîné	Entraîner suggests entail. School entails (provokes) work. The train is the part of the dress that flows behind, i.e. the train provoked by the main body of the dress.	Provoke
Entraîner	J'entraîne, j'ai entraîné	En**train**er suggests **train**	Train (other)
Entraîner, s'	Je m'emtraîne, Il s'entraîne, nous nous entraînons, ils s'entraînent, je m'entraînerai, je me suis entraîné	En**train**er suggests **train**, to train one**se**lf	Train (oneself)
Envoyer	J'envoie, il envoie, nous envoyons, ils envoient, j'enverrai, j'ai envoyé	A special **envoy** is a journalist who is sent to report on a dispute	Send
Épeler	J'épèle, j'ai épelé	É denotes 's' at the start of the word, i.e. **s**peler, spell	Spell
Épouser	J'épouse, j'ai épousé	É replaces 's' at the start of a word. Your spouse is your husband/wife.	Marry
Espérer	J'espère, j'ai espéré	De-**esper**ate is without hope	Hope

Word or phrase	Key forms of the verb	Aide-mémoire	English meaning	Check
Essayer	J'essaie, il essaie, nous essayons, ils essaient, j'essaierai, j'ai essayé	An **essa**y is a piece of written work where you **try** to present an idea	Try	
Éteindre	J'éteins, il éteint, nous éteignons, ils éteignent, j'éteindrai, j'ai éteint	**Étein**dre suggests **extin**guish	Switch off	
Être	Je suis, tu es, il est, nous sommes, vous êtes, ils sont, je serai, j'ai été (sois, soit, soyons, soient)	Ê denotes an 's', the **es**sence of life is being.	Be	
Être fort/faible	Je suis, tu es, il est, nous sommes, vous êtes, ils sont, je serai, j'ai été (sois, soit, soyons, soient)	Ê denotes an 's', the **es**sence of life is being. Fort – strong, like a fortress, fortitude is strength. Faible – link to feeble, weak.	Be, to be strong/weak	
Être au chômage	Je suis, tu es, il est, nous sommes, vous êtes, ils sont, je serai, j'ai été (sois, soit, soyons, soient)	Ê denotes an 's', the **es**sence of life is being, **ex**is**t**enc**e**. Chômage comes from chaud (warm). The Greek, 'caumare' meant to rest during the heat. We know 'chauffer' to warm, from the noun, chauffeur, a driver, employed to warm the car for his master. If we remember the link with heat and not working in it, we will remember unemployed.	Be unemployed	
Être d'accord	Je suis, tu es, il est, nous sommes, vous êtes, ils sont, je serai, j'ai été (sois, soit, soyons, soient)	Ê denotes an 's', the **es**sence of life is being, **ex**is**t**enc**e**. D' – of accord, to be of one accord, to agree. Musical chords are together in harmony.	Agree, to agree	
Être en retenue	Je suis, tu es, il est, nous sommes, vous êtes, ils sont, je serai, j'ai été (sois, soit, soyons, soient)	Ê denotes an 's', the **es**sence of life is being, **ex**is**t**enc**e**. Retenu – retained ('u' at the end of the word, denotes, -ed).	Detention, to be in detention	
Être collé	Je suis, tu es, il est, nous sommes, vous êtes, ils sont, je serai, j'ai été (sois, soit, soyons, soient)	Ê denotes an 's', the **es**sence of life is being, **ex**is**t**enc**e**. **Collé** – **coll**ar**ed**, to get collared (é – ed).	Detention, to be in detention	
Être dangereux	Je suis dangereux		Be dangerous	
Être occupé	Je suis occupé	Occupied	Be busy	
Être sociable	Je suis sociable		Be sociable	
Être timide	Je suis timide,	Timid	Be shy	
Étudier	J'étudie, j'ai étudié	É denotes an 's' at the start of the word, **s**tudy	Study	
Éviter	J'évite, j'ai évité	Sounds like avoid or evade	Avoid	
Exagérer	J'exagère, j'ai exagéré		Exaggerate	

LES VERBES LES PLUS IMPORTANTS

Word or phrase	Key forms of the verb	Aide-mémoire	English meaning	Check
Examiner	J'examine, j'ai examiné		Examine	
Faire	Je fais, tu fais, il fait, nous faisons, vous faites, ils font, je ferai, j'ai fait (fasse, fasses, fasse, fassions, fassiez, fassent)	**Fare**well, do well, how are you **far**ing, how are you doing, a feat is a thing done. Feasible means do-able; defeated is undone.	Do, make	
Faire correspondre	Je fais, tu fais, il fait, nous faisons, vous faites, ils font, je ferai, j'ai fait (fasse, fasses, fasse, fassions, fassiez, fassent)	**Fa**ire suggests **fa**bricate, manu**fa**cture, to make. Correspondre – correspond, to make correspond, to match.	Match	
Faire attention	Je fais, tu fais, il fait, nous faisons, vous faites, ils font, je ferai, j'ai fait (fasse, fasses, fasse, fassions, fassiez, fassent)	**Fare**well, do well, how are you **far**ing, how are you doing. Attention – in English, we pay attention, but in French, you do attention.	Attention, to pay, be careful	
Faire de la gymnastique	Je fais, tu fais, il fait, nous faisons, vous faites, ils font, je ferai, j'ai fait (fasse, fasses, fasse, fassions, fassiez, fassent)	**Fare**well, do well, how are you **far**ing, how are you doing. Gymnastique – gymnastics.	Gymnastics, to do	
Faire de la voile	Je fais, tu fais, il fait, nous faisons, vous faites, ils font, je ferai, j'ai fait (fasse, fasses, fasse, fassions, fassiez, fassent)	**Fare**well, do well, how are you **far**ing, how are you doing. Voile – link to veil, piece of cloth like a sail.	Sailing, to do	
Faire de l'équitation	Je fais, tu fais, il fait, nous faisons, vous faites, ils font, je ferai, j'ai fait (fasse, fasses, fasse, fassions, fassiez, fassent)	**Fare**well, do well, how are you **far**ing, how are you doing. **Equi**ne – link to horses. **Equ**es**trian** – link to horses.	Horse-riding, to do	
Faire de l'exercice	Je fais, tu fais, il fait, nous faisons, vous faites, ils font, je ferai, j'ai fait (fasse, fasses, fasse, fassions, fassiez, fassent)	**Fare**well, do well, how are you **far**ing, how are you doing. Exer**c**i**ce** – exerci**se**.	Exercise, to do	
Faire des achats	Je fais, tu fais, il fait, nous faisons, vous faites, ils font, je ferai, j'ai fait (fasse, fasses, fasse, fassions, fassiez, fassent)	**Fa**ire suggests **fa**bricate. Manu**fa**cture – to make. A**chat**s are pur**ch**ase**s**. A chat (cat) might be a purrrchase.	Shopping, to do the shopping (general household shopping)	
Faire des économies	Je fais, tu fais, il fait, nous faisons, vous faites, ils font, je ferai, j'ai fait (fasse, fasses, fasse, fassions, fassiez, fassent)	**Fa**ire suggest **fa**bricate. Manu**fa**cture – to make. To be economical is to save money. Make economies, make savings.	Save, to save money	

Word or phrase	Key forms of the verb	Aide-mémoire	English meaning	Check
Faire du sport	Je fais du sport, tu fais, il fait, nous faisons, vous faites, ils font, je ferai, j'ai fait (fasse, fasses, fasse, fassions, fassiez, fassent)	**Far**ewell, do well, how are you **far**ing, how are you doing. Sport – sport.	Sport, to do	
Faire du bénévolat	Je fais du bénévolat, il fait, nous faisons, vous faites, ils font, je ferai, j'ai fait (fasse, fasses, fasse, fassions, fassiez, fassent)	**Far**ewell, do well, how are you **far**ing, how are you doing. A feat is a thing done, feasible means do-able, defeated is undone. Benevolence is kindness without pay, volunteering	Volunteering, to do volunteering	
Faire beau	Il fait beau, il fera beau, (nous faisons beau) il a fait beau, subjunctive: (fasse, fasses, fasse, fassions, fassiez, fassent)	**Fa**ire – **fa**bricate, manu**fa**cture – to make. **Beau**tiful. It's making beautiful, it's nice weather.	Nice weather, to be nice weather	
Faire grève	Je fais grève, il fait, nous faisons, vous faites, ils font, je ferai, j'ai fait (fasse, fasses, fasse, fassions, fassiez, fassent)	**Grev**ious bodily harm is caused by **strik**ing someone. Une grève – an action to display one's **griev**ance.	Strike, to go on strike	
Faire mauvais	Il fait mauvais, il fera mauvais, (nous faisons mauvais) il a fait mauvais (fasse, fasses, fasse, fassions, fassiez, fassent)	**Fa**ire – **fa**bricate, manu**fa**cture – to make. **Ma**uvais, mal – bad. Malnutrition, malpractice etc. Vais – comes from aller, to go. **Va**(is) **va**(is) **voom**. It's going badly. It's making bad going, bad weather.	Bad weather, to be bad weather	
Faire la grasse matinée	Je fais la grasse matinée, il fait, nous faisons, vous faites, ils font, je ferai, j'ai fait (fasse, fasses, fasse, fassions, fassiez, fassent)	**Fa**ire – **fa**bricate, manu**fa**cture – to make. Grasse matinée – gras/grasse (greasy) fat. Matinée – early, morning showing at cinema. Faire la grasse matinée – to do the fat morning.	Lie in bed late	
Faire une croisière	Je fais une croisière, il fait, nous faisons, vous faites, ils font, je ferai, j'ai fait (fasse, fasses, fasse, fassions, fassiez, fassent)	**Far**ewell, do well, how are you **far**ing, how are you doing, a feat is a thing done, feasible means do-able, defeated is undone. **Cro**i**siè**re – **cr**u**iser**.	Cruise, to go on a cruise	
Faire la cuisine	Je fais la cuisine, il fait, nous faisons, vous faites, ils font, je ferai, j'ai fait (fasse, fasses, fasse, fassions, fassiez, fassent)	**Fa**ire – **fa**bricate, manu**fa**cture – to make. **C**uis**ine** – **co**o**k**ing, **ki**t**c**h**en**. Nouvelle cuisine is a classy style of cooking which focuses on quality and presentation, not quantity.	Cooking, to do the cooking	

LES VERBES LES PLUS IMPORTANTS

Word or phrase	Key forms of the verb	Aide-mémoire	English meaning	Check
Faire les courses	Je fais les courses, il fait, nous faisons, vous faites, ils font, je ferai, j'ai fait (fasse, fasses, fasse, fassions, fassiez, fassent)	Courses – courier. The idea is that someone is running around, getting items and delivering them (home).	Shopping (food), to do the shopping	
Faire le jardinage	Je fais le jardinage, il fait, nous faisons, vous faites, ils font, je ferai, j'ai fait (fasse, fasses, fasse, fassions, fassiez, fassent)	Jardin – garden	Gardening, to do the gardening	
Faire la lessive	Je fais la lessive, il fait, nous faisons, vous faites, ils font, je ferai, j'ai fait (fasse, fasses, fasse, fassions, fassiez, fassent)	**La**vatory, water, **lessive**, washing of clothes. Doing the **la**undry in a machine means I have 'lessive' it to do by hand.	Washing (clothes), to do the washing	
Faire le lit	Je fais le lit, il fait, nous faisons, vous faites, ils font, je ferai, j'ai fait (fasse, fasses, fasse, fassions, fassiez, fassent)	I **lit**erally **li**e down and close my eye**li**ds	Bed, to make the bed	
Faire le ménage	Je fais le ménage, il fait, nous faisons, vous faites, ils font, je ferai, j'ai fait (fasse, fasses, fasse, fassions, fassiez, fassent)	I m**anage** to do the housework. Un ménage à trois means a household of three people. Katie Perry sang about it!	Housework, to do the housework	
Faire le repassage	Je fais le repassage, il fait, nous faisons, vous faites, ils font, je ferai, j'ai fait (fasse, fasses, fasse, fassions, fassiez, fassent)	Pass your iron over your shirts, then re-pass, then re-pass again. That's it, they've been re-passed with the iron, ironed.	Ironing, to do the ironing	
Faire la vaisselle	Je fais la vaisselle, il fait, nous faisons, vous faites, ils font, je ferai, j'ai fait (fasse, fasses, fasse, fassions, fassiez, fassent)	The table was considered to be a **vessel** carrying all the utensils and crockery used for eating: plates, knives, forks, spoons etc. The vessel now means the utensils and crockery themselves. Faire la **vaisselle** (or laver la vaisselle) means to do the dishes.	Dishes, to do the dishes	
Faire partie de	Je fais partie de, il fait, nous faisons, vous faites, ils font, je ferai, j'ai fait (fasse, fasses, fasse, fassions, fassiez, fassent)	**Part**ie. **Fa**ire – **fa**bricate, manu**fa**cture – to make. Make part of, be part of.	Part of, be part of	
Falloir, il faut	Il faut, nous fallons, ils faillent	It **fa**ils otherwise	Be necessary (one must)	
Fermer	Je ferme, j'ai fermé	**Firm**ly shut	Shut	

Word or phrase	Key forms of the verb	Aide-mémoire	English meaning
Fêter	Je fête, j'ai fêté	A fête is a garden party. Also, fe**s**tival, fe**s**tivities. Remember that ê denotes 's' after ê.	Celebrate
Finir	Je finis, il finit, nous finissons, ils finissent, je finirai, j'ai fini	Finir – **fini**sh	Finish
Frire	Je fris, il frit, nous frions, ils frient, je frirai, j'ai frit	Frire links to fry. Frites, pommes de terre frit**es** (fem, **e**; pl, **s**), frites is literally translated as 'fried ones'.	Fry
Fumer	Je fume, j'ai fumé	**Fume**s	Smoke
Gagner	Je gagne, j'ai gagné	**Ga**in victory	Win
Gagner de l'argent	Je gagne, j'ai gagné	**Ga**in money, earn money. Argent means silver as well as money. (Argento is the name of a shop that sells silver.) Ag is the chemical symbol for silver, silver is money.	Earn money
Gagner des intérêts	Je gagne, j'ai gagné	**Ga**in interest. Remember that ê denotes 's' after ê.	Earn interest
Garder	Je garde, j'ai gardé	Garder – guard, keep	Keep
Gaspiller	Je gaspille, j'ai gaspillé	**Piller** like pillage, is wrecking for wrecking's sake, a waste. This activity releases waste **gas**.	Waste
Gâter	Je gâte, j'ai gâté	Spoilt with a big **gâte**au, or cake	Spoil
Geler	Je gèle, Il gèle, nous gelons, ils gèlent, je gèlerai, j'ai gelé	Gel is cold. Jelly freezes. Chilly, jelly, gel.	Freeze
Gêner	Je gêne, j'ai gêné	**Gen**uinely embarrassed. Going red is in the genes. Don't embarrass Jenny!	Embarass, bother
Goûter	Je goûte, j'ai goûté	**Dé**goûter – disgust, disgusting, distasteful. The opposite of disgust (distaste) is taste.	Taste
Graver	Je grave, j'ai gravé	En**grave** data onto a CD	Burn (CD)
Grimper	Je grimpe, j'ai grimpé	A **grap**pling iron is used to climb. **Grap**ple is the verb which means, 'to move upward', 'make progress' but to struggle while doing it, like climbing.	Climb
Habiter	J'habite, j'ai habité	In**habit**	Live
Hurler	J'hurle, j'ai hurlé	Earl's scream made my toes c**url**. And, stop **hurl**ing abuse at me!	Scream
Imprimer	J'imprime, j'ai imprimé	Making an impression is a printing term. The characters are pressed on to paper. This is called an **imp**ression – **impr**imer.	Print
Indiquer	J'indique, j'ai indiqué		Indicate

Word or phrase	Key forms of the verb	Aide-mémoire	English meaning	Check
Informer	J'informe, j'ai informé		Inform	
Insister	J'insiste, j'ai insisté		Insist	
Injurer	J'injure, j'ai injuré	He **injure**d my feelings with his insults	Insult	
Insulter	J'insulte, j'ai insulté		Insult	
Intégrer	J'intègre, j'ai intégré		Integrate	
Interrompre	J'interromps, il interrompt, nous interrompons, ils interrompent, j'interromprai, j'ai interrompu	Rompre – to break, gives us **rup**tu**re**, break the speech, looks like interrupt	Interrupt	
Intervenir	J'interviens, il intervient, nous intervenons, ils interviennent, j'interviendrai, je suis intervenu		Intervene	
Inviter	J'invite, j'ai invité		Invite	
Jeter	Je jette, il jette, nous jetons, ils jettent, je jeterai, j'ai jeté	A **jett**y is a platform thrown out into the lake. A plane **jett**isons excess fuel.	Throw away	
Jeûner	Je jeûne, j'ai jeûné	Déjeuner is breakfast, 'dé' reverses the meaning.	Fast	
Jouer	Je joue, j'ai joué	A **jo**y to play. **Jo**cular is playful.	Play	
Laisser	Je laisse, j'ai laissé	'Laissez-faire' politics is a policy of non-intervention, '**lea**ve to do', '**le**t happen'.	Leave (something somewhere), let	
Laisser tomber	Je laisse tomber, j'ai laissé tomber	**Le**t **tumb**le means to drop	Drop	
Lancer	Je lance, j'ai lancé	**La**un**c**h – **lanc**er. Launch means to throw, up in the air.	Throw	
Lier	Je lie, j'ai lié	**Li**er – **li**nk	Link	
Lire	Je lis, il lit, nous lisons, ils lisent, je lirai, j'ai lu	**L**ectu**re**	Read	
Livrer	Je livre, j'ai livré	Livrer is almost deliver.	Deliver	
Louer	Je loue, j'ai loué	**L**ou**er** suggests **le**nder. You rent from a lender.	Hire, rent	
Lutter	Je lutte, j'ai lutté	You **lu**nge at someone when you fight them, as you m**utter**, 'I'll get you!'	Fight	
Manger	Je mange, nous mangeons, ils mangent, je mangerai, j'ai mangé	Cattle eat from a **manger**	Eat	
Manquer de	Je manque de, j'ai manqué de	**M**iss out on, fail to do something. My monkey managed to miss his monk.	Fail to do (something)	

Word or phrase	Key forms of the verb	Aide-mémoire	English meaning
Manquer (à quelqu'un)	Je lui manque, je lui ai manqué	**M**iss – I miss my monkey, my monkey is missing to me – mon singe me manque.	Miss (someone)
Marcher	Je marche, J'ai marché	**March**ing is walking	Walk
Marcher	Ça marche, Ça a marché	Marching is a well-organised, well-balanced, unstoppable motion. It just keeps going, all in order, like a machine. Ça marche means, 'it works' as in 'it functions'.	Work (function)
Marginaliser	Je marginalise, j'ai marginalisé		Marginalise
Menacer	Je menace, nous menaçons, ils menacent, je menacerai, j'ai menacé	**Menac**er suggests **menac**ing	Threaten
Mentir	Je mens, il ment, nous mentons, ils mentent, je mentirai, j'ai menti	If you are **men**dacious, you are dishonest. You are **me**ant to tell the truth!	Lie, tell a lie
Mettre	Je mets, il met, nous mettons, ils mettent, je mettrai, j'ai mis	To e**mit** rays, to put out rays, to o**mit**, to fail to put something down, mention	Put, put on
Mettre en ligne	Je mets, il met, nous mettons, ils mettent, je mettrai, j'ai mis	To e**mit** rays, to **put** out rays, to o**mit**, to fail to **put** something down, mention. En ligne – line.	Put on line
Mettre la table	Je mets, il met, nous mettons, ils mettent, je mettrai, j'ai mis	To e**mit** rays, to **put** out rays, to o**mit**, to fail to **put** something down, mention. Here meaning to put (things on) the table.	Set the table
Monter	Je monte, je suis monté	Go up a **mount**ain	Go up
Mourir	Je meurs, il meurt, nous mourons, ils meurent, je mourrai, je suis mort	**Mor**gue, **mor**tuary, **mor**bid, **mour**ning all linked to death	Die
Nager	Je nage, nous nageons, ils nagent, je nagerai, j'ai nagé	**Na**vy, **na**utical, sea, swim	Swim
Naître	Je nais, il naît. Nous naissons, ils naissent, je naîtrai, je suis né(e)	**Na**tivity, birth of Jesus. On a mariage certificate, a woman's maiden name is marked as née, e.g. 'née Smith'.	Born, be
Neiger	Il neige, il a neigé	The **s**neige in winter nestles in the nooks and crevices. Sn**eig**e is good for a sl**eig**h.	Snow
Nettoyer	Je nettoie, il nettoie, nous nettoyons, ils nettoient, je nettoierai, j'ai nettoyé	**Net**toyer is to **ne**atify. Neat and clean are linked. Your **net** pay is what is left after your gross (dirty) pay is cleaned away.	Clean
Nuire à	Je nuis, il nuit, nous nuisons, ils nuisent, je nuirai, j'ai nui	**Nuis**ances are harmful	Harm

Word or phrase	Key forms of the verb	Aide-mémoire	English meaning	Check
Offrir	J'offre, il offre, nous offrons, ils offrent, j'offrirai, j'ai offert		Offer	
Organiser	J'organise, j'ai organisé		Organise	
Oublier	J'oublie, j'ai oublié	An oubliette, the name for a Norman dungeon, where people were forgotten. **Ou bl**ast I forgot!	Forget	
Ouvrir un compte	J'ouvre, il ouvre, nous ouvrons, ils ouvrent, j'ouvrirai, j'ai ouvert	An overt communist is someone who is very open about his/her beliefs. Un **com**p**t**e – ac**cou**nt.	Open an account	
Pagayer	Je pagaie, j'ai pagayé	**Pa**ddle, **pa**ddling **gu**y	Paddle	
Parler	Je parle, j'ai parlé	MPs speak to each other in **parl**iament. A **parl**our is a room designed for people to speak to each other.	Speak, talk	
Partager	Je partage, nous partageons, ils partagent, je partagerai, j'ai partagé	If you share something everyone has a 'part(ager)'	Share	
Participer à	Je participe, j'ai participé		Participate in	
Partir	Je pars, il part, nous partons, ils partent, je partirai, je suis parti	Depart ends in -part. Departure, leave.	Leave (as in the train leaves – **not** leave something somewhere or leave a place)	
Passer	Je passe, j'ai passé	Passtime, pass time, spend time	Spend time	
Passer	Je passe, j'ai passé		Pass (the salt)	
Passer un examen	Je passe un examen, j'ai passé	Passer contains the word **ass**, used for sitting	To **sit** an exam	
Passer l'aspirateur	Je passe l'aspirateur, j'ai passé	To **pass** the r**espirator** over the floor so that it sucks up (breathes in) dust	Vaccum clean, hoovering	
Patienter	Je patiente, j'ai patienté	To (be) patient	Wait patiently	
Patiner	Je patine, j'ai patiné	In English we are 'sk**atin**' but in French, we are 'p**atin**' (pronounced pah-tah, however).	Skate	
Payer en liquide	Je paie, nous payons, ils paient, je paierai, j'ai payé	A credit card is a solid. When you break it down, it is seen as liquid, cash.	Pay (for) in cash	
Payer par carte	Je paie, nous payons, ils paient, je paierai, j'ai payé	Par – by. Carte – card.	Pay by card	
Pêcher	Je pêche, j'ai pêché	If a person in government is im**peach**ed, they are caught out and removed from office (like fish taken from water).	Fish (go fishing)	

Word or phrase	Key forms of the verb	Aide-mémoire	English meaning	Check
Pécher	Je pèche, il pèche, nous péchons, ils pèchent, je pécherai, j'ai péché	Pécher is linked to im**peach**ment. If you sin in public office, you get impeached, removed from office.	Sin	
Peindre	Je peins, il peint, nous peignons, ils peignent, je peindrai, j'ai peint	**Peind**re – **pain**t	Paint	
Perdre	Je perds, il perd, nous perdons, ils perdent, je perdrai, j'ai perdu	Perdition (purgatory) is another word in English for 'hell', a place where one is 'lost'	Lose	
Perdre, se	Je me perds, tu te perds, il se perd, nous perdons, ils se perdent, je me perdrai, je me suis perdu	Perdition (purgatory) is another word in English for 'hell', a place where one is 'lost'	Get lost (lose one**se**lf)	
Permettre	Je permets, il permet, nous permettons, ils permettent, je permettrai, j'ai permis	Permit	Allow	
Plaindre	Je plains, il plaint, nous plaignons, ils plaignent, je plaindrai, j'ai plaint	**Pi** is slightly helpful. Also the past part of this verb, 'plain**t**' with the 't', helps	Pity	
Plaindre, se	Je me plains, tu te plains, il se plaint, nous nous plagnons, ils se plaignent, je me plandrai, je me suis plaint	A **plain**tif is someone who has a com**plaint**, with the 'se'. I am pitying my**se**lf if I am complaining.	Complain	
Plaire	Je plais, il plaît, s'il te plaît, s'il vous plaît, ça m'a plu	**Pla**ire link to **pl**e**a**se	Please	
Pleurer	Je pleure, j'ai pleuré	Pleurisy is a condition where you have water on the lung. **Pl**ip, **pl**ip, **pl**ip, teardrops from your eye.	Cry	
Pleuvoir	Il pleut, nous pleuvons, ils pleuvent, il pleuvra, il a plu	Pronunciation of pleut is 'pleuh', Think of 'pleuh', 'pleuh', 'pleuh', raindrops. Also 'pleurisy' is a condition which involves **flui**d (p**lui**e, rain) on the lungs.	Rain	
Polluer	Je pollue, j'ai pollué	**Pollu**er – **pollu**te	Pollute	
Porter	Je porte, j'ai porté	A porter carries stuff	Carry	
Porter	Je porte, j'ai porté	If you wear clothing, you are carrying it	Wear	
Poser	Je pose, j'ai posé	To pose a question is to put (ask) a question	Ask a question/ to set (put) down	
Poser sa candidature	Je pose ma candidature, j'ai posé ma candidature	Pose a question, put a question. Put down a candidacy. You put your name down as a candidate for a job, you apply for a job.	Apply for a job	
Posséder	Je possède, j'ai possédé		Possess, own	

LES VERBES LES PLUS IMPORTANTS

Word or phrase	Key forms of the verb	Aide-mémoire	English meaning	Check
Pouvoir	Je peux, tu peux, il peut, nous pouvons, ils peuvent, je pourrai, j'ai pu (puisse, puisses, puisse, puissions, puissiez, puissent)	**Po**we**r** is ability	Be able, can	
Pratiquer un sport	Je pratique, j'ai pratiqué		Sport, to do (practise) a	
Préférer	Je préfère, j'ai préféré		Prefer	
Prendre (le petit déjeuner)	Je prends, il prend, nous prenons, ils prennent, je prendrai, j'ai pris	Entre**prendre** means 'to under**take**', to undertake a project. From entreprendre, we have entrepreneur and une entreprise (an undertaking, business).	Take breakfast	
Préparer	Je prépare, j'ai préparé		Prepare	
Présenter	Je présente, j'ai présenté		Present, introduce	
Préserver	Je préserve, j'ai préservé		Preserve	
Prêter	Je prête, j'ai prêté	The 'ê' denotes an 's' after the 'e'. Hey presto, it's ready for you – I will loan it to you.	Loan	
Profiter de	Je profite, j'ai profité	Profit from something, make the most	Make the most of	
Produire	Je produis, il produit, nous produisons, ils produisent, je produirai, j'ai produit		Produce	
Profiter	Je profite, j'ai profité	Profit from is 'benefit from'	Benefit from	
Programmer	Je programme, j'ai programmé		Program	
Promener le chien	Je promène, il promène, nous promenons, ils promènent, je promènerai, j'ai promené	A promenade is a walkway by the beach	Walk the dog	
Promener, se	Je me promène, il se promène, nous nous promenons, ils prominent, je me promènerai, je me suis promené	A promenade is a walkway by the beach	Walk (myself)	
Prononcer	Je prononce, j'ai prononcé	Prononce – pronounce	Pronounce	
Proposer	Je propose, j'ai proposé		Propose, suggest	
Protéger	Je protège, il protège, nous protégeons, ils protègent, je protégerai, j'ai protégé		Protect	
Punir	Je punis, il punit, nous punissons, ils punissent, je punirai, j'ai puni		Punish	

Word or phrase	Key forms of the verb	Aide-mémoire	English meaning	Check
Quitter la maison	Je quitte, j'ai quitté	To quit cigarettes is to leave them behind. Quitter is always followed by a noun.	Leave (a place, person) the house	
Raconter	Je raconte, j'ai raconté	A raconteur is an English word for 'story-teller'. In English, one recounts a story.	Tell (story)	
Ranger	Je range, j'ai rangé	Ar**range** my bedroom, tidy my bedroom. 'Deranged' means crazy, disordered.	Tidy	
Rappeler	Je rappelle, j'ai rappelé	Appeler – to appeal, to call upon. Rappeler – to re-call, remind, to remind someone.	Remind	
Rapporter	Je rapporte, j'ai rapporté	Porters carry away, re**porter**s bring back information	Bring back	
Rassurer	Je rassure, j'ai rassuré		Reassure	
Rater	Je rate, j'ai raté	Miss and fail are negative words. What is the most negatively associated animal? You got it, the **rat**! He ratted on me and made me fail.	Miss, fail	
Reçevoir	Je reçois, il reçoit, nous recevons, ils reçoivent, je recevrai, j'ai reçu		Receive	
Recommander	Je recommande, j'ai recommandé		Recommend	
Récompenser	Je récompense, j'ai récompensé		Compensate	
Reculer	Je recule, j'ai reculé	Cul-de-sac means 'bum of bag'. Bum associated with rear or behind. Both of these are linked to going back and retreating.	Go back, retreat	
Redoubler	Je redouble, j'ai redoublé	You do the year once, you fail, so you redouble (do it again)	Repeat a year	
Réduire	Je réduis, il réduit, nous réduisons, ils réduisent, je réduirai, j'ai réduit		Reduce	
Regarder	Je regarde, j'ai regardé	If you say, 'regarding that' you mean 'looking at that'	Look at, watch	
Réintroduire	Je réintroduis, il réintroduit, nous réintroduisons, ils réintroduisent, je réintroduirai, j'ai réintroduit		Reintroduce	
Remercier	Je remercie, j'ai remercié	Merci – thank you	Thank	

LES VERBES LES PLUS IMPORTANTS

Word or phrase	Key forms of the verb	Aide-mémoire	English meaning	Check
Remettre (past participle: Remis)	Je remets, il remet, nous remettons, ils remittent, je remettrai, j'ai remis	If you are working on pre**mise**, you are working from an idea that has already been 'put' down, pre-put. 'Mis' is the past participle of mettre. Here the date is of the match is re-put to another day.	Put off (postpone) e.g. a match	
Remporter	Je remporte, j'ai remporté	The winner takes it all, literally. The prefix 'em-', as in **em**igrate, is 'away'. If you carry (porter) away (em) the prize, it is because you have won.	Win	
Rencontrer	Je rencontre, j'ai rencontré	To encounter someone is to meet them for the first time. To re-encounter is to meet up.	Meet	
Rendre visite à quelqu'un	Je rends visite, il rend, nous rendons, ils rendent, je rendrai, j'ai rendu visite	Render – 'you have rendered me a valuable service'. Se rendre – to give oneself in (surrender), to give a visit to someone.	To visit someone. Used to express a visit to a person	
Renforcer	Je renforce, j'ai renforcé	**Renforc**er – **re**i**nforc**e	Reinforce	
Rentrer	Je rentre, je suis rentré	To re-enter, go back home	Go home	
Renverser	Je renverse, j'ai renversé	To invert means to turn something upside down, which is like knocking it over	Knock over, knock down	
Réparer	Je répare, j'ai réparé	Réparer – link to repair	Repair	
Repasser	Je repasse, j'ai repassé	Pass the iron over clothes and re-pass until there are no folds	Iron (clothes)	
Répéter	Je répète, j'ai répété	Répéter suggests repeater. If you repeat, you rehearse.	Repeat, rehearse	
Répondre	Je réponds, il répond, nous répondons, ils respondent, je répondrai, j'ai répondu		Answer, respond	
Réserver	Je réserve, j'ai réservé		Reserve, book	
Résoudre	Je résous, il résout, nous résolvons, ils résolvent, je résoudrai, j'ai résolu	**Réso**udre – **reso**lve	Resolve	
Respecter	Je respecte, j'ai respecté		Respect	
Respire	Je respire, j'ai respire	Respiration, breathing, respirator, breathing machine	Breathe	
Rester	Je reste, je suis resté	If an apple does not roll off the table, it **rests** or **stays** on it	Stay	
Retenir	Je retiens, il reticent, nous retenons, ils retiennent, je retiendrai, j'ai retenu	To remember means to **retain** the information in your head	Remember	
Retourner	Je retourne, je suis retourné		Return	

27

Word or phrase	Key forms of the verb	Aide-mémoire	English meaning
Réussir	Je réussis, il réussit, nous réussissons, ils réussissent, je réussirai, j'ai réussi	Success and r**éuss**ir are close enough	Succeed, pass exam
Réveiller	Je réveille, j'ai réveillé	**Revi**ve	Wake up
Réveiller se	Je me réveille, il se réveille, nous nous réveillons, ils se réveillent, je me réveillerai, je me suis réveillé	**Revi**ve	Wake up (oneself)
Revenir	Je reviens, il revient, nous revenons, ils reviennent, je reviendrai, je suis revenu	Income, what comes back to you when you work, is your **reven**ue	Come back
Rêver	Je rêve, j'ai rêvé	To be lost in revery means to be lost in dreams. Dreaming of the **rev**olution!	Dream
Réviser	Je révise, j'ai révisé	**Révise**r – **revise**	Revise
Ridiculiser	Je ridiculise, j'ai ridiculisé		Ridicule
Rire	Je ris, il rit, nous rions, ils rient, je rirai, j'ai ri	You rire (rear) back when you laugh heartily. Try it.	Laugh
Risquer	Je risque, j'ai risqué		Risk
Rôtir	Je rôtis, il rôtit, nous rôtissons, ils rôtissent, je rôtirai, j'ai rôti	The ô denotes an 's' after the ô. Rostir – link to **ro**a**st**.	Roast
Sauver	Je sauve, j'ai sauvé	A saviour saves, **sauver**	Save (from disaster, not money)
Sauvegarder	Je sauvegarde, j'ai sauvegardé	**Sa**feguard	Protect, conserve
Savoir	Je sais, il sait, nous savons, ils savent, je saurai, j'ai su. (Sache, saches, sache, sachions, sachiez, sachent)	If you are 'a bit savvy', you know how to do things	Know how
Se baigner	Je me baigne, je me suis baigné	**Ba**the	Bathe self
Se brosser les dents Se brosser les cheveux	Je me brosse les dents, il se brosse, nous nous brossons, ils se brossent, je me brosserai, je me suis brossé, Je me brosse les cheveux…	**Bros**ser – **brus**h. Dents – dentist. Cheveux – 'She veut' avoir de beaux cheveux – She wants to have nice hair.	Brush teeth, Brush hair
Se concentrer	Je me concentre, il se concentre, nous nous concentrons, ils se concentrent, je me concentrerai, je me suis concentré	Concentrate one**self**	To concentrate

Word or phrase	Key forms of the verb	Aide-mémoire	English meaning
Se connecter	Je me connecte, Il se connecte, nous nous connectons, ils se connectent, je me connecterai, je me suis connecté		Connect/ log on
Se coucher	Je me couche, il se couche, nous nous couchons, ils se couchent, je me coucherai, je me suis couché	Lie on the couch!	Lie down
Se couper	Je me coupe, il se coupe, nous nous coupons, ils se coupent, je me couperai, je me suis coupé	A car called a 'coupé' is one that can have no roof. The roof has been **cut** off.	Cut self
Se déconnecter	Je me déconnecte, il se déconnecte, nous nous déconnectons, ils se déconnectent, je me déconnecterai, je me suis déconnecté	To **disconnect** myself	Log off
Se déplacer	Je me déplace, je me suis déplacé	Déplacer – to move. **Displace**.	Move about
Se déshabiller	Je me déshabille, il se déshabille, nous nous déshabillons, ils se déshabillent, je me déshabillerai, je me suis déshabillé	A monk's habit is his cloak (dress). The 'de' as a prefix reverses the meaning. So **déshabi**ller – undress.	Undress
Se distraire	Je me distrais, je me suis distrait	To **distra**ct oneself is to amuse oneself	Amuse self
Se doucher	Je me douche, je me suis douché	'Douche' is the sound of a bucket of water being emptied on your head	Shower self
S'efforcer	Je m'efforce, je me suis efforcé	**Effor**t	Try (make effort)
S'engager	Je m'engage, il s'engage, nous nous engageons, ils s'engagent, je m'engagerai, je me suis engagé	Engage one**sel**f in, to join up in	Join up
S'entendre avec	Je m'entends avec, il s'entend, nous nous entendons, ils s'entendent, je m'entendrai, je me suis entendu avec	Entendre – to h**ear**. An '**enten**te' (an agreement) comes when people listen to each other, hear each other.	Get on well with
S'entraîner	Je m'entraîne, je me suis entraîné	**Train**	Train oneself

Word or phrase	Key forms of the verb	Aide-mémoire	English meaning	Check
Se faire des amis	Je me fais des amis, il se fait, nous nous faisons, vous vous faites, ils se font, je me suis fait, je me ferai	**Fa**ire – **fa**bricate, manu**fa**cture	Make friends (for oneself)	
S'habiller	Je m'habille, je me suis habillé	A monk's **habi**t is his clothing	Get dressed	
S'identifier	Je m'identifie, il s'identifie, nous nous identifions, ils s'indentifient, je m'identifierai, je me suis identifié	Identify oneself	To log in	
S'inquiéter	Je m'inquiète, je me suis inquiété	When you are not at peace with yourself, you are not quiet with yourself, you are u**nquiet**, you are worried	Worry	
S'inscrire	Je m'inscris, il s'inscrit, nous nous inscrivons, ils s'inscrivent, je m'inscrirai, je me suis inscrit	To inscribe one's name on a list, to sign up	To sign up, to register	
S'installer	Je m'installe, je me suis installé	Install yourself, settle down	Settle down	
S'instruire	Je m'instruis, il s'instruit, nous nous instruisons, ils s'instruisent, je m'instruirai, je me suis instruit	**Instru**ct yourself, teach yourself	Teach self	
S'intéresser à	Je m'intéresse, je me suis intéressé	Interest yourself in something	Be interested in (also means to 'fancy' a person)	
Se laver	Je me lave, je me suis lavé	**Lav**atory, water, washing	Wash self	
Se lever	Je me lève, je me suis levé	**Lev**itate, e**lev**ate, lift up, get up	Get self up	
Se maquiller	Je me maquille, il se maquille, nous nous maquillons, ils se maquillent, je me maquillerai, je me suis maquillé	**Ma**nne**qui**ns wear make-up. During the German occupation of France, the Resistance were called the Maquis. They camouflaged themselves. Like when one uses make-up.	Make oneself up (apply make-up)	
Se marier	Je me marie, je me suis marié		Marry	
Se mettre en colère	Je me mets en colère, il se met, nous nous mettons, ils se mettent, je me suis mis, je me mettrai	**Col**ère – **col**ic makes babies angry. Se mettre – to put oneself. ('metteur en scène' is a film producer, a 'putter on scene').	To get angry (to put oneself angry)	
Se passionner pour	Je me passionne pour, je me suis passionné pour,	Be **passion**ate about something is being really interested	Be really interested	
Se préoccuper de	Je me préoccupe, je me suis préoccupé	Preoccupied links to worried	Worry	
Se raser	Je me rase, il se rase, nous nous rasons, ils se rasent, je me raserai, je me suis rasé	Razor for shaving	Shave	

Word or phrase	Key forms of the verb	Aide-mémoire	English meaning
Se rappeler	Je me rappelle, je me suis rappelé	Appeler – to appeal, to call upon. Rappeler – to re-call, remind, to remind oneself, to remember.	Remember
Se rencontrer	On se rencontre, On s'est rencontré	To encounter someone is to meet them. **Re**en**co**unter is to meet up again.	Meet up
Se reposer	Je me repose, je me suis reposé	**Resp**ite is **r**e**s**t, **rep**o**s**er. To de**pos**it is to lay something down. To re**pose** on**self** is to lie down and take **res**t.	Rest
Se retrouver	Je retrouve, j'ai retrouvé	Trouver – treasure **trove**, a treasure find, to find each other again (re), to meet.	Meet up
Se sentir	Je me sens, il se sent, nous nous sentons, ils se sentent, je me sentirai, je me suis senti	To s**en**se danger, to have a **sen**sation, to feel	Feel (abstract, e.g. sad, happy)
Se situer	Je me situe, je me suis situé		Be situated
Se soûler	Je me soûle, je me suis soûlé	The û denotes an 's' after the u. 'é' denotes -ed. To get sousled, sossled, sozzled drunk.	Drunk, to get drunk
Se souvenir de	Je me souviens de, il se souvient, nous nous souvenons, ils se souviennent, je me souviendrai, je me suis souvenu de	A souvenir is to remind you of something	Remember
Se taire	Je me tais, il se tait, nous nous taisons, ils se taisent, je me tairai, je me suis tu	A **ta**cit understanding is an un-spoken understanding. **Ta**citurn – not talkative.	Fall silent (say nothing)
Sécher	Je sèche, j'ai séché	When you are feeling '**sec**' (sick), you have a dry mouth, like after a training '**sech**ion'.	Dry
Sécher les cours	Je sèche, j'ai séché	When you are feeling '**sec**' (sick), you have a dry mouth, like after a training '**sech**ion'. Hey, you are still skipping classes! I'm sorry. I'm **drying** my best not to!	Skip classes
Sélectionner	Je sélectionne, j'ai sélectionné	**Sélect**ionner	Select
Sembler	Je semble, j'ai semblé	**Sembl**ance, re**sembl**ance	Seem
Sensibiliser	Je sensibiliser, j'ai sensibilisé	To appeal to people's **sens**e, make them take an idea on board, aware. **Sensi**tise.	Make aware
Séparer	Je sépare, j'ai séparé		Separate
Servir	Je sers, il sert, nous servons, ils servent, je servirai, j'ai servi		Serve
Siffler	Je siffle, j'ai sifflé	Wh**iffle**, onomatopeia	Whistle

Word or phrase	Key forms of the verb	Aide-mémoire	English meaning	Check
Soigner	Je soigne, j'ai soigné	Pronounced, 'swan-yeah'. If you **swo**on, you need cared for. I will **swing** by and care for you.	Take care of (heal)	
Sonner	Je sonne, j'ai sonné	To **so**und	Ring	
Sortir	Je sors, il sort, nous sortons, ils sortent, je sortirai, je suis sorti	You want to go out? Come with me, it's **sort**ed! A 'sortie' made by a jet fighter is an **out**ing, a flight.	Go out	
Sortir les poubelles	Je sors, il sort, nous sortons, ils sortent, je sortirai, je suis sorti	You want to **go out**? Come with me, it's **sort**ed! A 'sortie' made by a jet fighter is an **out**ing, a flight. Here we are not going out, but **bringing out**. Poubelle – bin, it poos, smells pooey. Ironic that belle, meaning beautiful comes after. It poos beautifully.	Bring out the bins	
Souffrir	Je souffre, il souffre, nous souffrons, ils souffrent, je souffrirai, j'ai souffert	Je souffre – suggests I suffer	Suffer	
Souhaiter	Je souhaite, j'ai souhaité	'À tes souhaits!' is the French equivalent of 'Bless you!' It is used in the poem, 'Ring a ring o' rosies.' We say, 'A tissue, A tissue!' It replaces 'Bless You, Bless You'. French was popular at the time of the Black Plague which this rhyme dates from. Also, I **wish** it wasn't so 'souhaiter' (hot in here).	Wish	
Sourire	Je souris, il sourit, nous sourions, ils sourient, je sourirai, j'ai souri	You rear (**rire**) back when you laugh). S**ou**s – under (**su**b-marine, underwater). Under your laugh, there is a smile.	Smile	
Stationner	Je stationne, j'ai stationné	Station**a**ry means immobile. To park is to make stationary.	Park	
Suivre	Je suis, il suit, nous suivons, ils suivent, je suivrai, j'ai suivi	To pur**sue**, is to follow. To follow to the courts is to **sue** someone.	Follow	
Surfer	Je surfe, j'ai surfé	Surfer link to surf	Surf	
Surveiller	Je surveille, j'ai surveillé	To survey a situation is to keep an eye on, look after	Look after	
Taper	Je tape, j'ai tapé	Type – taper	Type	
Taper	Ça tape	It is very warm. It's tapping (hitting) my head because it is so warm.	Hot weather	
Télécharger	Je télécharge, j'ai téléchargé	Charger suggests cargo, a load. To 'charge' your glass means to fill your glass. 'Tele' is Greek, meaning 'from a distance'. Load from a distance, i.e. download.	Download	

LES VERBES LES PLUS IMPORTANTS

Word or phrase	Key forms of the verb	Aide-mémoire	English meaning	Check
Tomber	Je tombe, je suis tombé(e)	Tomber – suggests to tumble, fall	Fall	
Tomber en panne	Je tombe en panne, je suis tombé en panne	Tomber, **tumb**le, fall, break-down. Panne – pain, difficulty	Break down, stop functioning	
Téléphoner à	Je téléphone, j'ai téléphoné		Telephone (to)	
Terminer	Je termine, j'ai terminé	Terminate – bring to an end. Get off at the terminus, the end.	End, finish	
Toucher	Je touche, j'ai touché	Touched with madness, affected by madness. 'Touché!' in English means, 'You got me!' (i.e. your comment stuck a chord, it affected or touched me).	Touch, affect	
Traduire	Je traduis, j'ai traduit	**D**u**ire** – diction, to say. **Tra**nsfer words, translate.	Translate	
Traîner	Je traîne, j'ai traîné	**Traî**ner suggests **trai**l. To trail, drag your feet, is to hang about, hang out with.	Trail, drag, hang about, hang out	
Traiter	Je traite, j'ai traité		Treat	
Travailler (dur)	Je travaille, j'ai travaillé	**Travai**ls in English are hardships in working. **Tria**ls are also demands at work. Dur – durable, hard. Work hard.	Work (hard)	
Traverser	Je traverse, j'ai traversé	To traverse is to cross, used with traversing a mountain or a desert	Cross	
Trier	Je trie, j'ai trié	A **tri**age nurse at A&E sorts through patients to see who needs the most help	Sort through	
Trouver	Je trouve, j'ai trouvé	A treasure **trove** is a discovery of treasure, a find	Find	
Trouver, se	Il se trouve, ils se trouvent	A treasure **trove** is a discovery of treasure, a find	Find itself, i.e. to be situated	
Tuer	Je tue, j'ai tué	Ma**tar** is Spanish for 'to kill', as in matador, killer of bull. This links to to **tuer**. In a war, '**t**o **er**r' (tuer) is to get yourself killed.	Kill	
Utiliser	J'utilise, j'ai utilisé	Utilise	Use	
Vendre	Je vends, il vend, nous vendons, ils vendent, je vendrai, j'ai vendu	A **vend**ing maching, a **vend**or of a house	Sell	
Venir	Je viens, il vient, nous venons, ils viennent, je viendrai, je suis venu	Come to a **ven**ue	Come	

Word or phrase	Key forms of the verb	Aide-mémoire	English meaning	Check
Venir de faire (quelque chose)	Je viens de, (je venais de)	Revenu is what comes back to you when you work. I am coming from doing something (have just done it). E.g: Je viens de manger – I have just eaten; Je venais de manger – I had just eaten.	Have just done something (had just done something)	
Verifier	Je vérifie, j'ai vérifié	To verify is to check	Check	
Visiter	Je visite, j'ai visité		Visit (e.g. a monument)	
Vivre	Je vis, il vit, nous vivons, ils vivent, je vivrai, j'ai vécu	**Viv**acious is **viv**id is full of life. C'est la vie – that's life.	Live	
Voir	Je vois, il voit, nous voyons, ils voient, je verrai, j'ai vu	A **vo**yeur is a Peeping Tom. A **v**iew is with your eyes.	See	
Voler	Je vole, j'ai volé	A **vol**ley is a kick in the air, to make it fly. A vol-au-vent is made with airy, light pastry, so it flies in the wind (vent).	Fly	
Voler	Je vole, j'ai volé	A voleur is a person who steals things of 'valeur' value	Steal	
Vomir	Je vomis, il vomit, nous vomissons, ils vomissent, je vomirai, j'ai vomi	**Vomi**r – **vomi**t	Vomit	
Vouloir	Je veux, tu veux, il veut, nous voulons, ils veulent, j'ai voulu (je veuille, nous voulions, ils veuillent)	I **volu**nteer because I want to do it	Want	
Vouloir dire	Je veux dire, j'ai voulu dire	To want (a **volu**nteer wants) to say (**di**ction). What does, 'chien' want to say? 'Chien' wants to say 'dog'. 'Chien' means 'dog'.	Mean	
Voyager	Je voyage, nous voyageons, ils voyagent, je voyagerai, j'ai voyagé	Voyage	Travel	

2: La colle française (les connecteurs)
French glue (the connectors)

Word or phrase	Pronunciation guide	Aide-mémoire	English meaning	Check
Beaucoup (de)	boh-kouh (deuh)	'A coup de' something – an amount of something. Beau coup, a nice (beautiful) amount of.	A lot (of)	
À propos de	ah proh-poh deuh	À propos de ma mère – **Approp**riate of my mum. About my mum.	About	
D'après	dah-pray	According to Daphne, 'Daddy, dab ray' was said by Dapper Dave	According to	
Selon	seuh-law	According to Ze-law, Ceylon is called Sri Lanka	According to	
Après	ah-pray	**A**près, **a**fter	After	
Encore/ de nouveau	awe-kore/ deuh nouh-voh	'Encore' is said at the end of a concert. 'De nouveau' means of new, a new attempt, i.e. again.	Again	
Il y a trois ans	eel-ee-ah trwaz-awe	There are (Il y a) three years (since that happened)	Ago (Three years ago)	
D'accord	dah-kohr	Of one accord	Agreed	
Tout/s (m)	touh	The **tot**ality of something is **all** of something	All	
Toute/s	touh-t (like toot but more hollow)	Tutti frutti, all the fruits	All	
Déjà	day-zhah	Déjà vu – already seen	Already	
Aussi	oh-see	**A**ussi - **a**lso	Also	
Bien que	bee-yeah keuh	I don't like him, although Bianca (bien que) does	Although	
Toujours	touh-zhouhr	All the days, tou(les)jours. Always is basically the same as 'alldays'.	Always	
Et	ay	'**Et** tu Brute?' ('**And** you Brutus?') – from the play Julius Caesar, by Shakespeare	And	
De toute fa**çon**	deuh touh-t fah-saw	Of all **fac**ets/**fac**ades. Of all ways to look at it. Anyway.	Anyway	
Comme	kawm	Comme Comme to the Somme **like**, **as** did many of our young Belfast men.	As, like	
Aussi... que	oh-see ... keuh	**Au**ssi has the same letters	As... as	
Autant de... que	oh-taw deuh ... keuh	Tant – so much. Ma tante fume tant! My aunt (tante) smokes so much. Stick 'au' in front of tant (autant), and use the 'a' of 'au' and we have **as much**/**as many as**.	As many as...	
Ainsi que	ah-see... keuh	Alison **as well as** Ashlea! **Ah**, **see** what I mean?	As well as	
D'abord	dah-bohr	À bord – on board. 'At the moment of boarding' is 'at first'.	At first	

Word or phrase	Pronunciation guide	Aide-mémoire	English meaning	Check
À (en) ce moment là	ah (awe) seuh moh-maw lah		At that moment	
À la fin	ah lah fah	Finish, fin, end	At the end	
En ce moment	awe seuh moh-maw		At the moment	
Lors de	lohr-deuh	'Lors de' sounds like 'l'heure de', the hour of, the time of	At the time of	
À cause de	ah kohze deuh	Literally means – 'at cause of'	Because of	
Parce que	paahr-seuh-keuh	Say this a few times – 'Parce que, parce que, parce que, because it just is!'	Because	
Avant	ah-vaw	A**dvan**ce parties go before the rest	Before	
D'ailleurs (de & ailleurs)	dye-yeuhr	Ailleurs – elsewhere. D'alleurs – of elsewhere, which means 'besides'. Besides, you shouldn't d'ailleurs hair.	Besides	
Les deux	lay deuh	The two (duo)	Both	
Mais	may	His butt, her butt, mais butt	But	
De près	deuh pray	If you are **pres**sed up against something you are very close to it	Closely	
Par rapport	paahr rah-pohr	A good rapport is a good connection with. Here, e.g. 'La Jaguar est chère par rapport à la Ford' – 'The Jaguar is expensive, in connection with the Ford'. In English we say, 'compared to'.	Compared	
Mot (m) de liaison	moh deuh lee-ay-zaw	Mot – word. Turn the M upside down and you have Wo like **Wo**rd. A liaison is a connection, normally in love but here it means a connection in words.	Connective	
Malgré	mal-gray	Gré – grace. Mal(bad)gré – **not** accepting it **grace**fully, in bad grace. 'Malgré le temps il est sorti' – 'Despite the weather, he went out'.	Despite	
Pendant	pawn-daw	While the **pend**ulum swings is something that happens during the swinging of the **pend**ulum	During	
Chacun(e)	shah-kah(koon)	**Ch**ac un – ea**ch** one (**ch**aq**ue** has the letters of 'each')	Each one	
Chaque	shak	**Ch**aque/ea**ch** (**ch**aq**ue** has the letters of 'each')	Each	
Soit... soit	swah... swah	'Soit X soit Y' – 'Either X or Y'. Note that it is two words, as in English.	Either... or	
Assez de	ah-say deuh	I am wading up to my **ass**ez in water. I have enough water!	Enough	
Surtout	soohr-touh	Sur – on/above (surhumain – super/abovehuman). This allows us to understand **sur** (above) **tout** (all). This links to 'above all' or 'especially'.	Especially (above all)	

LA COLLE FRANÇAISE (LES CONNECTEURS)

Word or phrase	Pronunciation guide	Aide-mémoire	English meaning	Check
Même si	mem see	'Même' and 'even' are the same length and both have two 'e's. Si has 50% of if!	Even if	
Jamais	zhah-may	Have you **ever** heard of that **Jammy** Jimmy Jamison?	Ever	
Tous les jours	touh lay zhouhr	Literally 'total of the days'. We know jour from 'bon jour', which means 'good day'. Total of the days means 'every day'.	Every day	
Tout le monde	touh leuh mawnd	Total of the **mound** of Earth that we call the world. Total of the world, all the world, everyone.	Everyone	
Sauf	sohff	**Sa**uf – **saf**e – **sa**ve. I leave all the sheep outside **except**, **save** this one.	Except	
Hormis	oar-mee	Hors – out. Mis – put. Hormis – put out. 'Tous hormis un' means 'all except (put out) one'.	Except	
extrêmement	eks-trem-euh-maw		Extremely	
Peu de	peuh deuh	**P**eu is linked to **p**altry, **p**oor. These words point to a small amount, few.	Few	
Car	kaahr	C**ar** links to f**or**, when 'for' means 'because'	For (because)	
Par exemple	paahr eks-awm-pleuh	As per example	For example	
Pour	pouhr	'Je suis à l'école pour apprendre' – 'I'm at school **for** (p**our**) to learn.'	For (purpose)	
À jamais	ah zha-may	Have you **ever** heard of that **Jammy** Jimmy Jamison? Here, **à** jamais means **to** ever, i.e. forever.	Forever	
Pour toujours	pouhr touh-zhouhr	P**our** –f**or**. **Tou**(t) **jours** – the total of the days. Forever.	Forever	
Dorénavant	dohr-ray-nah-vaw	'En avant' – forward. Open the **dor** and from this moment forward.	From now on	
Désormais	days-ohr-may	From now on. Remember the three syllables – days oar may (dés/or/mais).	From now on	
À partir de maintenant	ah paahr-teer deuh man-teuh-naw	De**part** – leave. De – from. Main – hand. Tenant – held out. Hand out, pay **now**! Leaving from now (on).	From now on	
Étant donné que	ay-taw daw-nay keuh	Étant – being (from être, to be). Donné – given (link to **don**ation, **don**or, give).	Given that	
Ne…guère	neuh…gair	Ne – gives us the negative element. 'Je ne vois guère la mer' – 'I can hardly see the sea'.	Hardly	
Qu'est ce que c'est bien!	kess-keuh say bee-yeah	Literally means 'What is it that it is good?' It is like the English expression, 'How good is that?'	How good!	
Qu'est ce que c'est nul!	kess-keuh say noohl	Literally means 'What is that it is rubbish?' It is like the English expression, 'How rubbish is that?'	How rubbish!	

37

Word or phrase	Pronunciation guide	Aide-mémoire	English meaning	Check
Toutefois	touht (like toot but more hollow) fwah	'Toute fois' literally means 'all times'. For example 'Il est coléreux. Toutefois il sait rire.' – 'He is firey. However (all times) he can laugh'.	However	
Pourtant	pouhr-taw	'Ma tante fume tant! Pour (for) tant (so much) elle est athlète'. – 'My aunt smokes so much! For so much (despite this) she's an athlete.'	However	
Cependant	seuh-pawn-daw	Ce – this. Ce is in the well-known phrase, C'est – this, or it is. 'Ce pendant' – 'during this'. There is a war on. During this (however) we try to laugh.	However	
Je venais de finir	zheuh ven-ay deuh fee-neer	Venir, venue – come to a venue. I was coming from finishing. I had just finished.	I had just finished	
Je viens de finir	zheuh vee-yeah deuh fee-neer	Venir, venue – come to a venue. I am coming from finishing. I have just finished.	I have just finished	
Si	see	Si – if. Two very small words. An 'i' is in both of them.	If	
Aussitôt	oh-see-toh	**Au**ssi – as. Tôt – early. The ô denotes an 's' after the o. **To**ast, for **early** morning. As early as possible is immediately.	Immediately	
En tout cas	awe touh kah	Literally means 'in total (of) cases'	In any case	
En fait	awe fet	En fait is very close to 'in fact'	In fact	
A mon avis	ah mawn ah-vee	À mon avis – to my ad**vi**ce	In my opinion	
En dépit de	awe day-pee deuh	Dépit suggests despite. Despite something is the same as 'in spite of'.	In spite of	
Y compris	ee kawm-pree	**Compr**ehensive means all inclusive. Y – there. **Y compris** – included there.	Including	
Au lieu de	oh lee-yeuh deuh	Lieu (place) tenant (holder) – placeholder. A Lieutenant holds, is in charge of the place). Au **lieu** de – à la **place** de – in **place** of – **instead** of.	Instead of	
Juste trois	zhoost trwah	Trio, three	Just three	
Moins de... que	mwah deuh... keuh	**Moins** – **minus**. Il fait **moins** 3 – it's **minus** 3. It is 3 less than 0.	Less... than	
Comme	kawm	Comme Comme to the Somme **like**, **as** did many of our young Belfast men.	Like, as	
Enclin à	awe-klah	**Inclin**ed to do something, likely to do something	Likely to	
Un peu de	ah peuh deuh	**P**eu is linked to **p**altry, **p**oor. These words point to a small amount.	Little (a little, a little bit)	
Peut-être que	peuht-et-reuh keuh	Peut-être – il peut être – it can be, it may be	Maybe	
Si ça se trouve	see sah seuh trouhve	Literally means 'if it finds itself'. Maybe, if things find themselves like this. A treasure trove is a treasure find. 'Si ça se trouve, on gagnera' – 'maybe we'll win'.	Maybe	

LA COLLE FRANÇAISE (LES CONNECTEURS)

Word or phrase	Pronunciation guide	Aide-mémoire	English meaning	Check
Ça pourrait être bien	sah pouh-ray et-reuh bee-yeah	**Pou**voi**r** – linked to **po**we**r**, linked to ability, can, might. Mighty (powerful).	Might be good (that…)	
Plus de… que	plooh deuh … keuh	Plus – more of… than	More… than	
Presque	press-keuh	Presque, pres … que. In the **pre**cinct, near. In my **pres**ence, near.	Nearly	
Ensuite	awe-sweet	En suite bathroom is **next** to your bedroom. You pur**sue**, you follow, come **next**.	Next	
Puis	pwee	I did this and next (then) I did that. It was all **pwee**-planned you know!	Next (list of actions)	
Prochain(e) (l'année)	proh-shah/ proh-shen	Ap**proa**ch (**proch**ain), to come near, to come **next** to.	Next (year)	
Maintenant	mahn-teuh-naw	Main – hand. **Man**ipulate is to **hand**le. Tenant **hold**s the house. Hand outheld. Pay now!	Now	
D'accord	dah-kohr	We are of one **accord**. We agree. Agreed, OK.	Ok	
Évidemment	ay-vee-deuh-maw	Evidently is obviously. The evidence is all there. It is clear.	Obviously	
Bien s**û**r	bee-yeah soohr	Bien – good, well, **ben**efit, **ben**efactor, **ben**evolent. Well sure! It is of course!	Of course	
Bien entendu	bee-yen awn-tawn-doo	Bien – good, well, **ben**efit, **ben**efactor, **ben**evolent. Well understood! ('en ten du' and 'un der stood' have the same number of syllables, and sound a little alike, of course.)	Of course	
Souvent	souh-vaw	Souvent and often are linked. Look at them: same syllables, same letters, s**o**u**vent**. You will accept that a 'v' is like an 'f'.	Often	
De la part de (de ma part)	deuh lah pahr deuh	Literally means 'on the part of (Jill)' – on Jill's behalf. De ma part – on my part, on my behalf.	On behalf of (on my behalf)	
D'une part	doon pahr	On one part, on one hand	On one hand	
D'autre part	doat-reuh pahr	On other part, on the other hand (autre and other are clearly linked)	On the other hand	
Par contre	pahr kawn-treuh	By (on) the **contr**ary, on the other hand	On the other hand	
Ne… que	neuh… keuh	'Ne' gives us the negative element. 'Je ne mange que les légumes'. I only eat vegetables.	Only	
Ou	ouh	Ou – or	Or	
Le seul	leuh seuhl	The solitary person – la seule personne. The only person.	The only	
Peut-être	peuh-ett-reuh	Peut comes from pouvoir, to be able. (Pouvoir, power, ability). Peut être – can be.	Perhaps	
Assez	ah-say	Assez bien – quite good. Same number of letters in each word. Ah, say, 'It's quite good!'	Quite	
Vrai	vray	Verity is truth. Truth is real.	Real	

Word or phrase	Pronunciation guide	Aide-mémoire	English meaning
Vraiment	vray-maw	C'est **vrai** – it is **true**, it is **real.** Putting -ment on the end creates an adverb, -ly.	Really
Par rapport à	pahr rah-pohr ah	Rapport – relationship. 'Par rapport à' – 'per relationship to', which means regarding.	Regarding
Même	mem	Same – même	Same
Vu que	voo keuh	Vu, view, seen that	Seeing that
Puisque	pweese keuh	Pu**is**que – **si**nce, meaning because. It looks like 'parce que', which also means because.	Since (because)
Depuis qu'il est arrivé	deuh pwee keuh	De – from. Puis – then. De puis – from then, since. Since he arrived.	Since (plus a phrase)
Depuis	deuh-pwee	Je fume depuis trois ans – I am smoking since (for) three years	Since (for)
Alors	ah-lohr	À l'heure – at the hour. J'avais fini alors je suis sorti. – I'd finished so (at that time) I went out.	So (next)
Si	see	So suggests si. Si splendide – so spendid.	So (really)
Tellement	tel-maw	I'll **tell** me **maw** when I get home that the boys are SO annoying. Tellement pénible!	So (really)
Donc	donk	Je pense donc je suis – I think therefore I am.	So (therefore)
Tant que	taw keuh	Literally means, 'so much as'. For example, Je resterai tant que tu resteras – I will stay so long (so much) as you will stay.	So long as (so much as)
Tant de...	taw deuh	Tant – so much. Ma tante fume tant de cigarettes! – My aunt (tante) smokes so many cigarettes!	So many
Pour que	pouhr keuh	**Pour que** je puisse – **so that** I can. Give him a lie test so that he can't tell **pour ques**!	So that
Quelqu'un	kell-kah	Quelque – some. Un – one.	Someone
Quelque chose	kell-keuh shows	Quelque – some. Chose – thing. 'Cosa nostra' is the Mafia's motto, meaning, 'Our (nostra) thing (cosa)'. 'Cosa' is the Latin word that gives us 'chose' in French. I chose a thing with the same number of letters. It shows!	Something
Quelque(s)	kell-keuh	Say this phrase a few times: 'Some kell-keuh would help yeuh!' Keep saying it and remember some!	Some
Quelque fois	kell-keuh fwah	Quelque – some. Fois – times. La première fois que j'ai joué, j'ai gagné – Fwah!	Sometimes
Dès que...	day keuh	As soon as the day (dès) breaks. Dès que Desmond peut – As soon as Desmond can.	As soon as...
Le début	leuh day-boo	A début is a start. A debutant is a beginner, someone who is starting.	Start
Toujours	touh-zhouhr	Tout – total. Jours – days. Toujours – total (of the) days. On and on. Still.	Still

LA COLLE FRANÇAISE (LES CONNECTEURS)

Word or phrase	Pronunciation guide	Aide-mémoire	English meaning	Check
De tels commentaires	deuh tel kawm-maw-tair	Tel/s (telle/s) – means 'such' when it is in front of a noun. Such comments. Telling comments. Such a **tell**ing word!	Such comments	
Que	keuh	Tu es plus grande **que** moi – You are taller than me.	Than	
Que	keuh	Tu es la personne **que** j'adore – You are the person **that I** (the do-er of the action) adore.	That (connector, precedes a do-er of action)	
Qui	kee	Tu es la personne **qui** comprend – You are the person **that understands** (verb).	That (connector, precedes a verb)	
Ça	sah	Ça va? Literally means, 'that goes?'	That (do-er of action)	
C'est pour ça que je l'aime	say pouhr sah keuh zheuh lem	Literally means, 'It is (c'est) for that that I like it.'	That's why I like it	
C'est-à-dire	say-tah-deer	C'est – that is. **Di**re – **di**ction, **di**ctionary, words, things that we say.	That is to say	
alors	ah-lohr	À l'heure (alors), at the hour. J'avais fini alors je suis sorti – I'd finished **then** (at that time) I went out.	Then	
Ceci	seuh-see	Ce (i)ci. Ce – this. Ici – here. 'This here'.	This (can be subject or object)	
Cela	seuh-lah	Cela. Ce – that. Là – there. 'That there'.	That (can be subject or object)	
Ce/cet/cette	seuh/set	Ce garçon (m), cet arbre (m, starts with a vowel), cette fille (f) – this boy, that tree, that girl	This/that (demonstrative adjective)	
Ces	say	Ces garçons, ces arbres, ces filles – these boys, these trees, these girls.	These/those (demonstrative adjective)	
Ainsi	ah-see	Je travaille et ainsi, j'apprends – I work and thus, (in this way) I learn. **Ah-see** what I mean? In **that way** you do!	Thus (in this, that way)	
Trop de	troh deuh	**Tr**o**p** – **to**o (much). Trop d'argent – too much money, trop de bonbons – too many sweets.	Too much/many	
Aussi	oh-see	Person A: Je t'aime! Person B: Je t'aime **aussi**! – Person A: I love you! Person B: I love you **too**! **Oh see** that I love you **too**!	Too	
Jusqu'à	zhoose-kah	Jus**qu**'à – up to (qu – up). Just up to or until.	Until	
Jusqu'à ce que	zhoose kass keuh	Jus**qu**'à – up to (qu – up). Just up to or until. Jusqu'à ce que je puisse – until I can.	Until + phrase	
Très	tray	Très bien! – very good!	Very	

Word or phrase	Pronunciation guide	Aide-mémoire	English meaning	Check
Ce qui est bien est	seuh kee ay bee-yeah ay	Literally means – 'that which is good is'	What is good is	
Ce qui me plaît est	seuh kee meuh play ay	That which **is (a verb)** pleasing to me	What is pleasing to me is	
Ce que tu dois faire est	seuh keuh too dwah fair ay	That which **you (a do-er of action)** have to do is	What you must do is	
Ce que j'aime est	seuh keuh zhem ay	That which I like is	What I like is	
Peu importe	peuh am-portt	Little importance, like whatever. Whatever the cost (little importance the cost).	Whatever	
Quand	kaw	'Tell me when will you be mine? Tell me cuando cuando cuando.' This is a song by Englebert Humperdinck. 'Cuando' is a Spanish word like the French word 'quand'.	When (connector and question)	
Lorsque	lohrss-keuh	Lors (from l'heure) que. Therefore, 'the hour that', or when.	When (connector)	
Tandis que	tawn-deese keuh	Il m'aime **tandis que** je ne l'aime pas – He loves me **whereas** I don't love him. I realise that there is no mnemonic here but maybe that makes it memorable!	Whereas/whilst	
Si	see	Si – if (meaning whether). If (whether) I want to or not – si je veux ou pas.	Whether	
Avec	ah-vek	Avec moi – with me. Avec Alek – with Alek.	With	

LA COLLE FRANÇAISE (LES CONNECTEURS)